Wooden Houses

WOODEN HOUSES

J.O. WENGSTRÖMS
MEKANISKA SNICKERI FABRIK
STOCKHOLM

PAVILIONS, BATHINGHOUSES, BALCONIES.

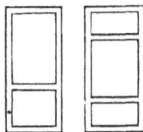

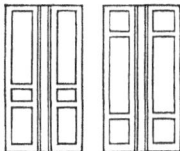

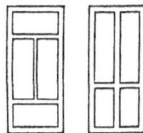

VERANDAS, DWELLINGHOUSES, KIOSKS.

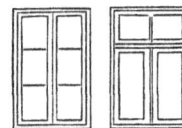

MANUFAKTURERS

— o OF o —

Wooden Houses.

DOORS, WINDOWS, ARCHITRAVES, SASHES, SKIRTINGS, MOUILDINGS.

PARQUETRY FLOORS
OF OAK, OF DIFFERENT DESIGNS.

Fredonia Books
Amsterdam, The Netherlands

Wooden Houses

by
J. O. Wengströms

ISBN: 1-58963-980-4

Fredonia Books
Amsterdam, The Netherlands
http://www.fredoniabooks.com

AKTIEBOLAGET
J.O.WENGSTRÖMS
MEK.SNICKERIFABRIK.
STOCKHOLM.

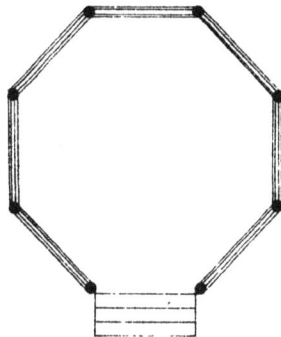

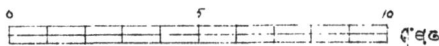

0   5   10

AKTIEBOLAGET
J.O.WENGSTRÖMS
MEK.SNICKERIFABRIK
STOCKHOLM.

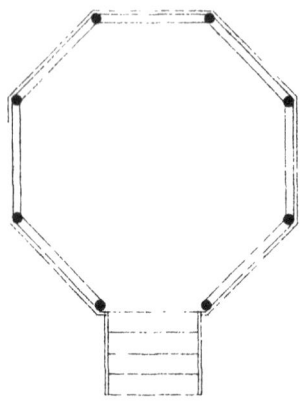

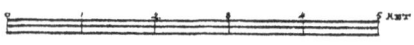

TRADE MARK

AKTIEBOLAGET
J.O. WENGSTRÖMS
MEK. SNICKERIFABRIK
STOCKHOLM.

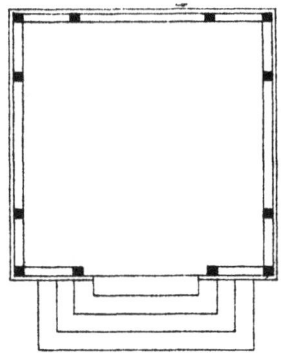

AKTIEBOLAGET
J.O.WENGSTRÖMS
MEK. SNICKERIFABRIK
STOCKHOLM.

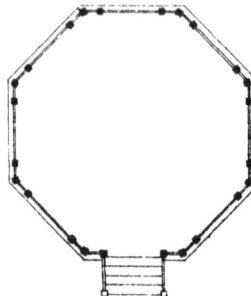

AKTIEBOLAGET
J. O. WENGSTRÖMS
MEK. SNICKERIFABRIK
STOCKHOLM.

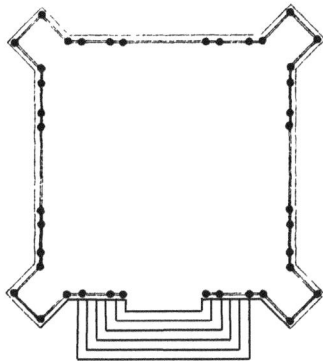

PL. 6.

AKTIEBOLAGET
J.O.WENGSTRÖMS
MEK. SNICKERIFABRIK
STOCKHOLM.

TRADE MARK

AKTIEBOLAGET
J.O.WENGSTRÖMS
MEK. SNICKERIFABRIK
STOCKHOLM.

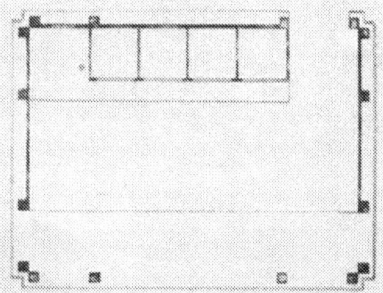

PL. 8.

AKTIEBOLAGET
J.O. WENGSTRÖMS
MEK. SNICKERIFABRIK
STOCKHOLM.

TRADE MARK

AKTIEBOLAGET
J.O.WENGSTRÖMS
MEK. SNICKERIFABRIK
STOCKHOLM.

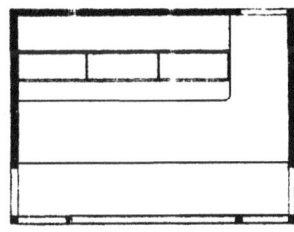

MET

AKTIEBOLAGET
J.O.WENGSTRÖMS
MEK. SNICKERIFABRIK
STOCKHOLM.

AKTIEBOLAGET
J.O.WENGSTRÖMS
MEK.SNICKERIFABRIK
STOCKHOLM.

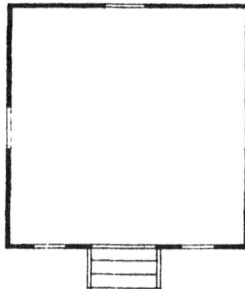

AKTIEBOLAGET
J.O.WENGSTRÖMS
MEK. SNICKERI FABRIK
STOCKHOLM.

TRADE MARK

AKTIEBOLAGET
J.O.WENGSTRÖMS
MEK. SNICKERIFABRIK
STOCKHOLM.

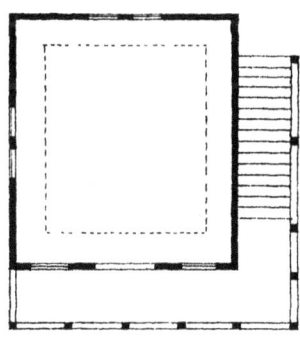

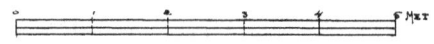

AKTIEBOLAGET
J.O.WENGSTRÖMS
MEK. SNICKERIFABRIK
STOCKHOLM

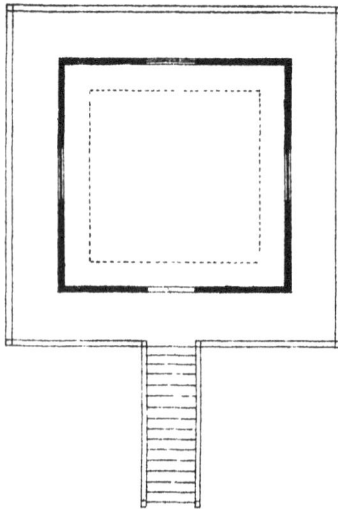

AKTIEBOLAGET
J. O WENGSTRÖMS
MEK. SNICKERIFABRIK
STOCKHOLM

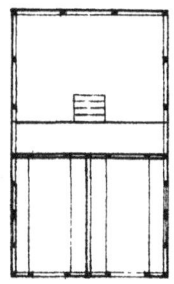

AKTIEBOLAGET
J.C.WENGSTRÖMS
MEK. SNICKERIFABRIK
STOCKHOLM.

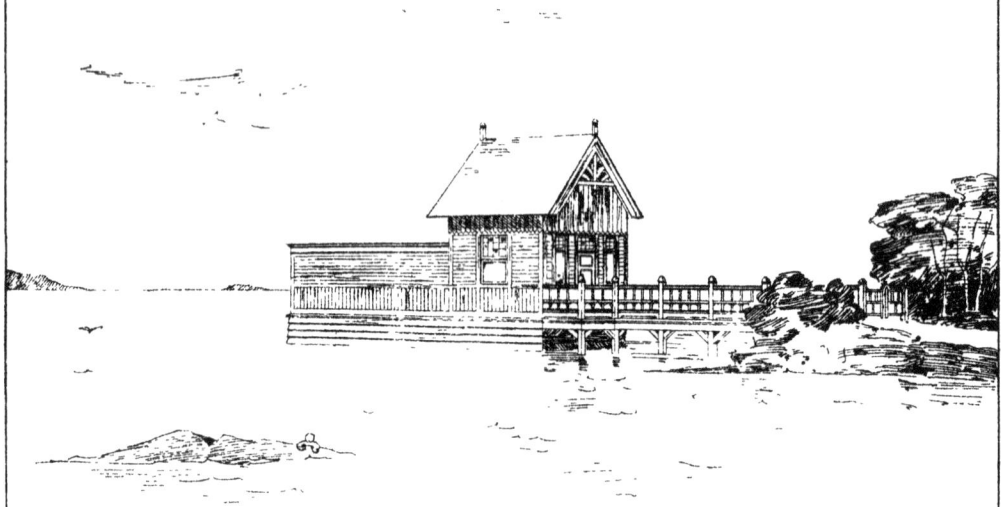

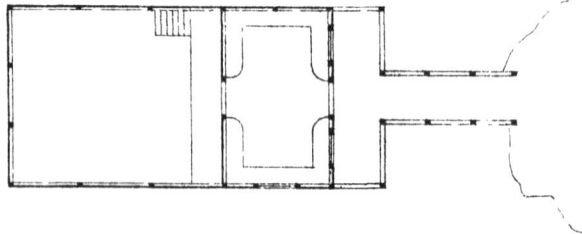

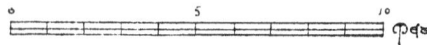

0   5   10 fot

AKTIEBOLAGET
J.O. WENGSTRÖMS
MEK. SNICKERIFABRIK
STOCKHOLM.

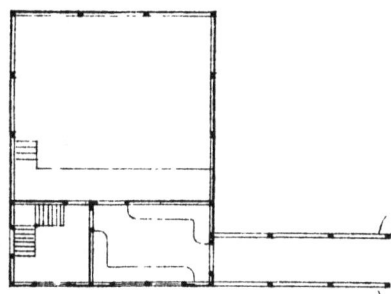

TRADE MARK

0   5   10 MET

AKTIEBOLAGET
J.O.WENGSTRÖMS
MEK. SNICKERIFABRIK
STOCKHOLM.

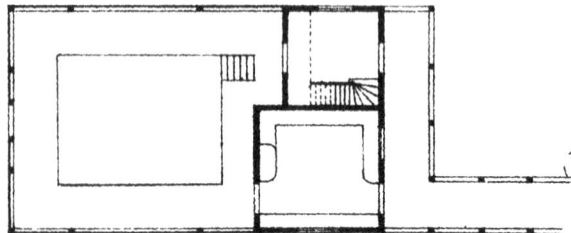

AKTIEBOLAGET
J.O.WENGSTRÖMS
MEK. SNICKERIFABRIK
STOCKHOLM.

AKTIEBOLAGET
J. O. WENGSTRÖMS
MEK. SNICKERIFABRIK
STOCKHOLM.

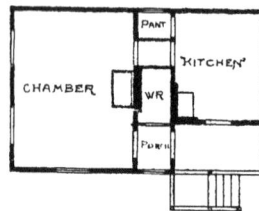

AKTIEBOLAGET
J.O.WENGSTRÖMS
MEK.SNICKERIFABRIK
STOCKHOLM.

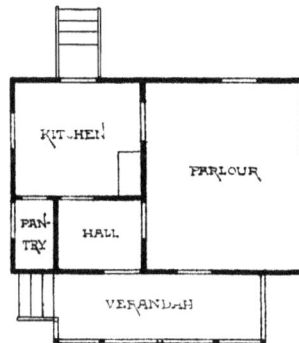

TRADE MARK

KITCHEN	PARLOUR
PAN-TRY	HALL
VERANDAH	

PL. 22

AKTIEBOLAGET
J.O.WENGSTRÖMS
MEK.SNICKERIFABRIK
STOCKHOLM.

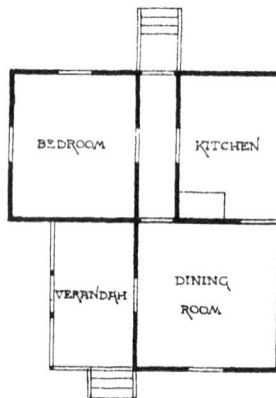

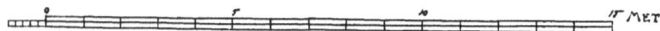

TRADE MARK

BEDROOM   KITCHEN

VERANDAH   DINING
ROOM

0   5   10   15 MET

PL 23.

AKTIEBOLAGET
J.O.WENGSTRÖMS
MEK SNICKERIFABRIK
STOCKHOLM.

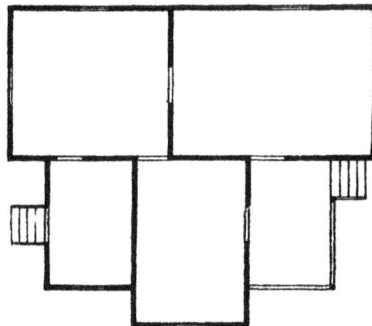

Meter

AKTIEBOLAGET
J.O. WENGSTRÖMS
MEK. SNICKERIFABRIK
STOCKHOLM.

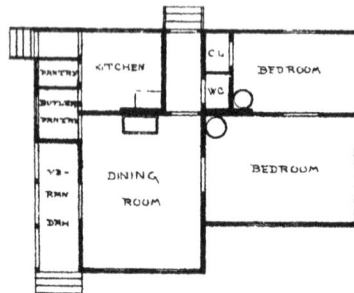

TRADE MARK

KITCHEN

PANTRY

BUTLERS
PANTRY

CL

WC

BEDROOM

VB-
RMN

DRH

DINING
ROOM

BEDROOM

MET

AKTIEBOLAGET
J.O. WENGSTRÖMS
MEK. SNICKERIFABRIK
STOCKHOLM.

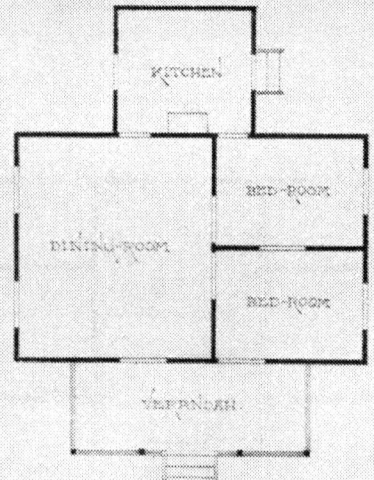

KITCHEN

BED-ROOM

DINING-ROOM

BED-ROOM

VERANDAH.

PL. 26

AKTIEBOLAGET
J.O.WENGSTRÖMS
MEK. SNICKERIFABRIK
STOCKHOLM.

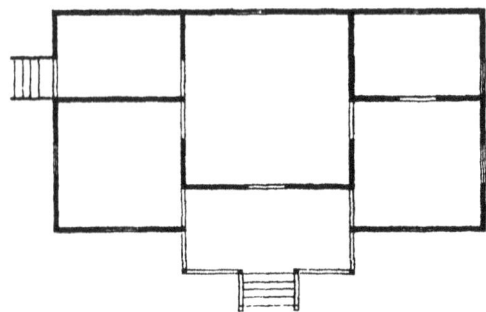

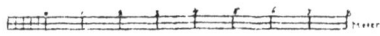

TRADE MARK

AKTIEBOLAGET
J.O. WENGSTRÖMS
MEK. SNICKERIFABRIK
STOCKHOLM.

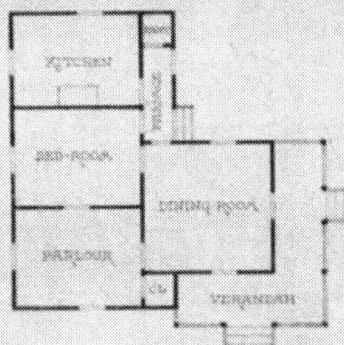

PL. 28.

AKTIEBOLAGET
J.O.WENGSTRÖMS
MEK. SNICKERIFABRIK
STOCKHOLM.

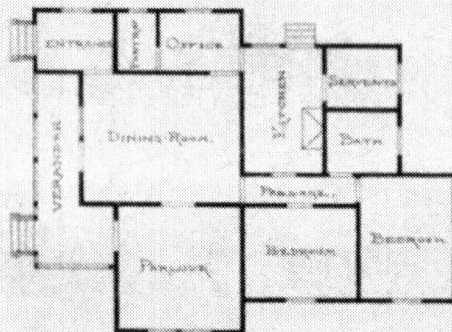

PL. 29.

AKTIEBOLAGET
J.O.WENGSTRÖMS
MEK. SNICKERIFABRIK
STOCKHOLM.

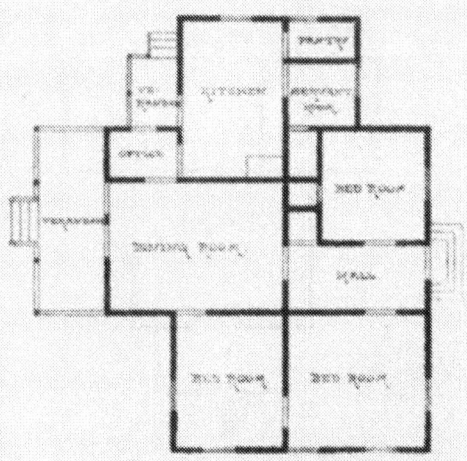

AKTIEBOLAGET
J.O.WENGSTRÖMS
MEK. SNICKERIFABRIK
STOCKHOLM.

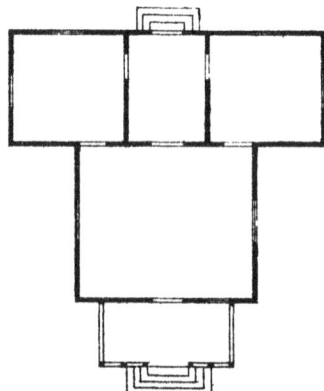

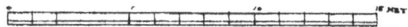

AKTIEBOLAGET
J.O.WENGSTRÖMS
MEK. SNICKERIFABRIK
STOCKHOLM.

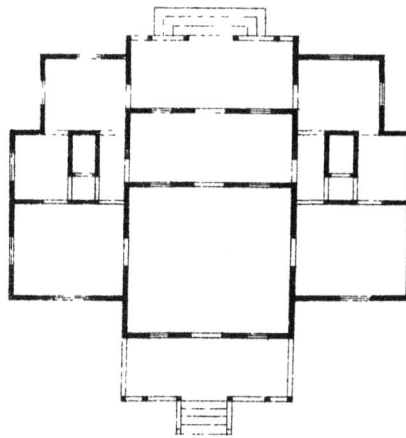

LAWN TENNIS PAVILION

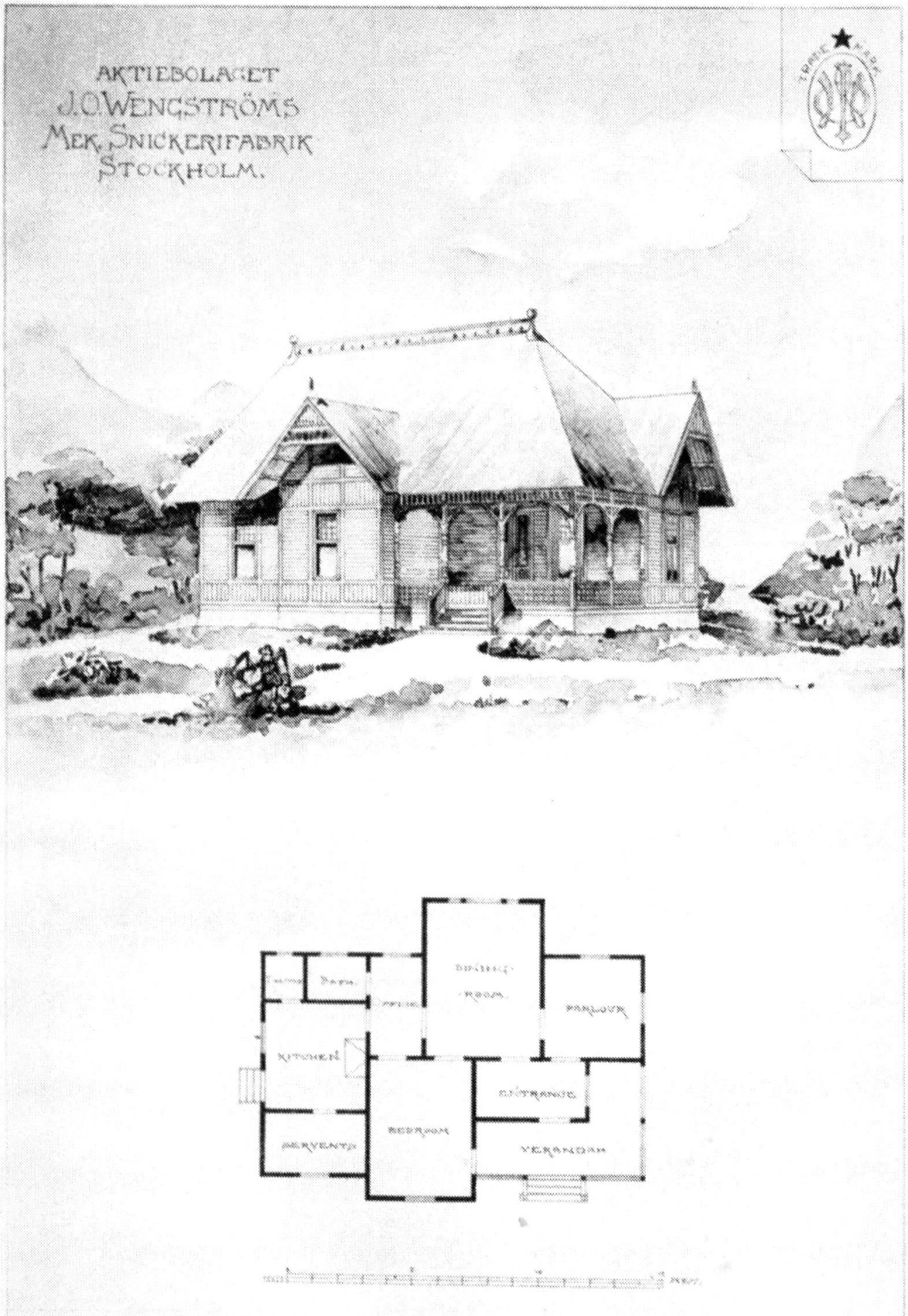
AKTIEBOLAGET
J. O. WENGSTRÖMS
MEK. SNICKERIFABRIK
STOCKHOLM.
KITCHEN
BEDROOM
SERVANTS
ENTRANCE
VERANDAH
PARLOUR
ROOM

PL. 33

AKTIEBOLAGET
J.O.WENGSTRÖMS
MEK. SNICKERIFABRIK
STOCKHOLM.

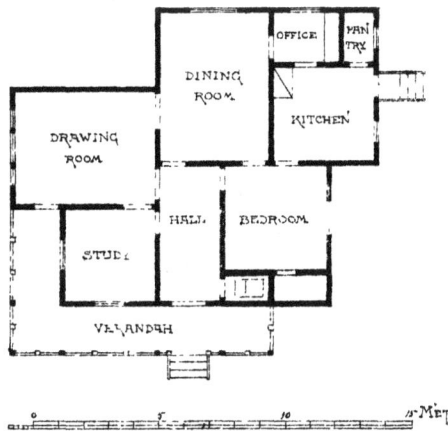

OFFICE | PANTRY
DINING ROOM
KITCHEN
DRAWING ROOM
HALL | BEDROOM
STUDY
VERANDAH

AKTIEBOLAGET
J.O.WENGSTRÖMS
MEK. SNICKERIFABRIK
STOCKHOLM

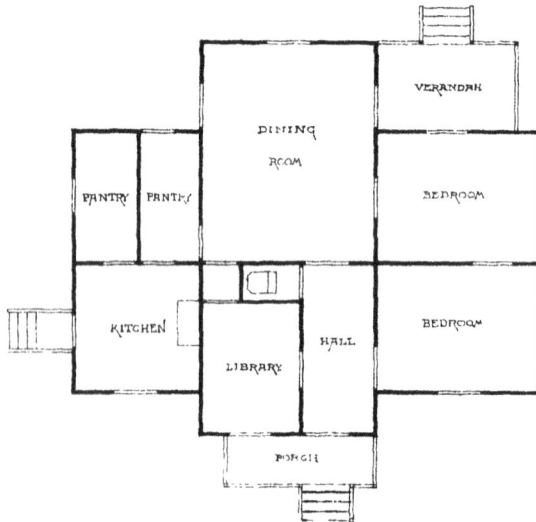

TRADE MARK

VERANDAH

DINING
ROOM

PANTRY | PANTRY

BEDROOM

KITCHEN

LIBRARY | HALL

BEDROOM

PORCH

AKTIEBOLAGET
J.C.WENGSTRÖMS
MEK. SNICKERIFABRIK
STOCKHOLM.

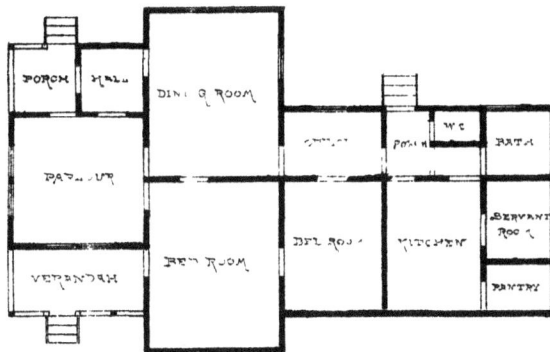

TRADE MARK

PORCH · HALL · DINING ROOM

PARLOUR

CLOSET · PORCH · W.C. · BATH

BED ROOM · BED ROOM · KITCHEN · SERVANT ROOM

VERANDAH · PANTRY

PL.36.

AKTIEBOLAGET
J.O.WENGSTRÖMS
MEK.SNICKERIFABRIK
STOCKHOLM.

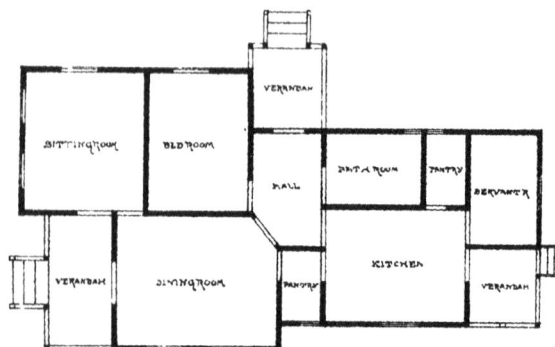

AKTIEBOLAGET
J.O.WENGSTRÖMS
MEK. SNICKERIFABRIK
STOCKHOLM.

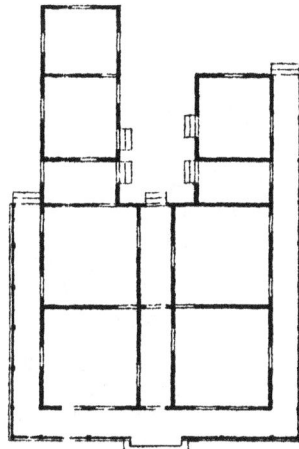

Pl. 38.

AKTIEBOLAGET
J.O.WENGSTRÖMS
MEK. SNICKERIFABRIK
STOCKHOLM.

TRADE MARK

Pl. 38.

TRADE MARK

AKTIEBOLAGET
J.O.WENGSTRÖMS
MEK. SNICKERIFABRIK
STOCKHOLM.

KITCHEN

PORCH

PORCH

BED R

BED R

BED R

BATH R

CL

SITTING R

DINING R

SITTING R

PORCH

BED R

BED R

CL

CL

BED R

BED R

CL

CL

BED R

SITTING R

SITTING R

BED R

PORCH

SITTING R

PORCH

BED R

BATH R

CL

BED R

AKTIEBOLAGET
J.O.WENGSTRÖMS
MEK. SNICKERIFABRIK
STOCKHOLM.

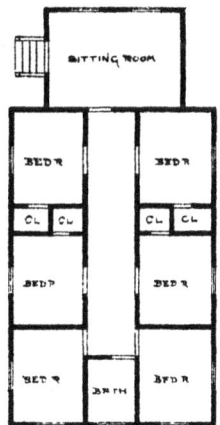

SITTING ROOM

BED R | BED R

CL | CL | CL | CL

BED R | BED R

BED R | BATH | BED R

0   5   10   15 MET

AKTIEBOLAGET
J.O.WENGSTRÖMS
MEK. SNICKERIFABRIK
STOCKHOLM.

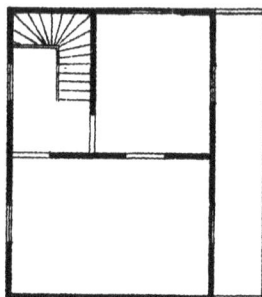

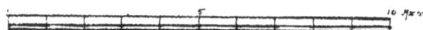

10 MET.

AKTIEBOLAGET
J.O.WENGSTRÖMS
MEK. SNICKERIFABRIK
STOCKHOLM.

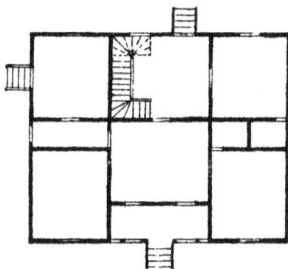

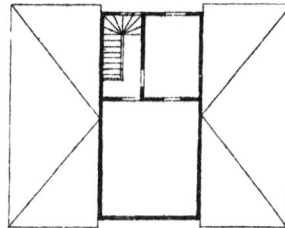

AKTIEBOLAGET
J.O.WENGSTRÖMS
MEK. SNICKERIFABRIK
STOCKHOLM.

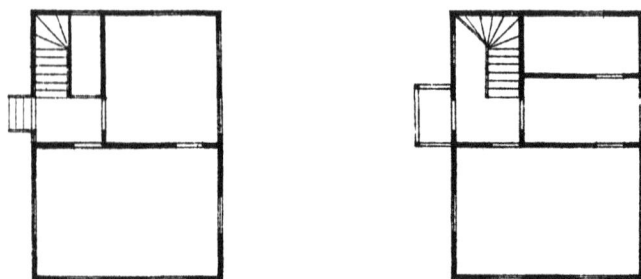

AKTIEBOLAGET
J.O.WENGSTRÖMS
MEK. SNICKERIFABRIK
STOCKHOLM.

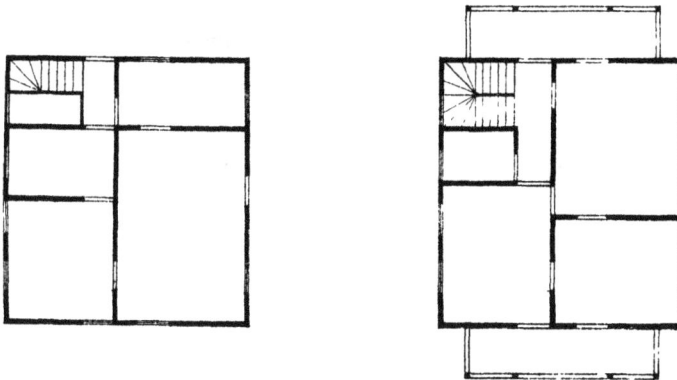

AKTIEBOLAGET
J.O.WENGSTRÖMS
MEK. SNICKERIFABRIK
STOCKHOLM.

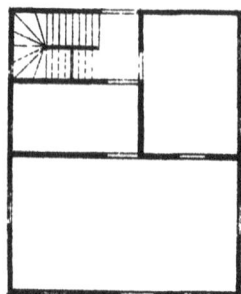

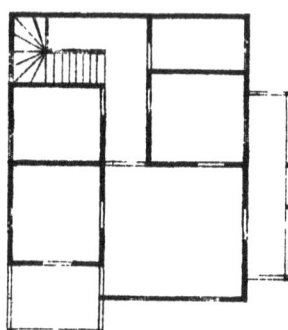

AKTIEBOLAGET
J.O.WENGSTRÖMS
MEK. SNICKERIFABRIK
STOCKHOLM.

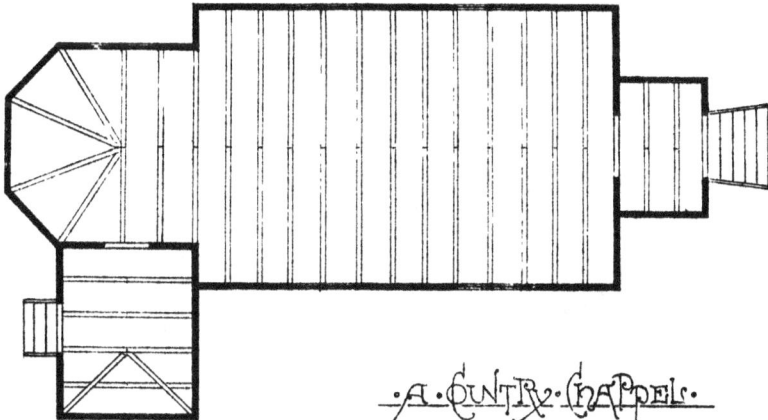

·A·COUNTRY·CHAPPEL·

AKTIEBOLAGET
J.O.WENGSTRÖMS
MEK. SNICKERIFABRIK
STOCKHOLM.

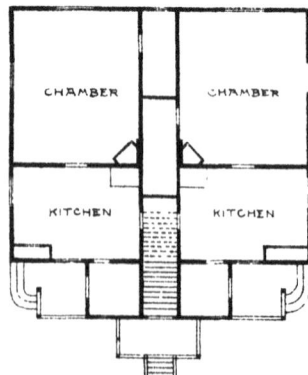

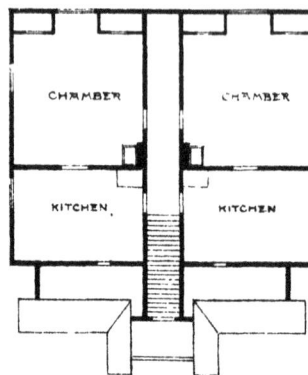

CHAMBER	CHAMBER
KITCHEN	KITCHEN

CHAMBER	CHAMBER
KITCHEN.	KITCHEN

5   10   15 MET

AKTIEBOLAGET
J.O.WENGSTRÖMS
MEK. SNICKERIFABRIK
STOCKHOLM.

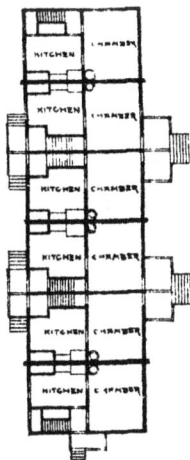

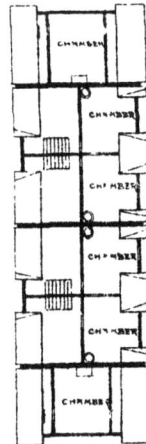

Pl. 48.

AKTIEBOLAGET
J.O.WENGSTRÖMS
MEK. SNICKERIFABRIK
STOCKHOLM.

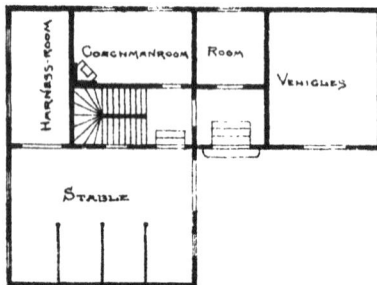

TRADE MARK

HARNESS-ROOM | COACHMANROOM | ROOM | VEHICLES

STABLE

Pl. 42.

AKTIEBOLAGET
J.O. WENGSTRÖMS
MEK. SNICKERIFABRIK
STOCKHOLM.

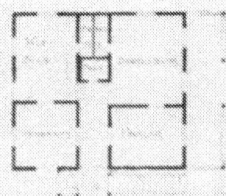

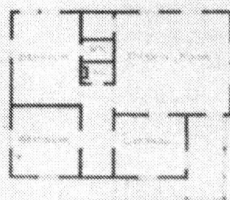

PLs.50.

AKTIEBOLAGET
J.O.WENGSTRÖMS
MEK. SNICKERIFABRIK
STOCKHOLM.

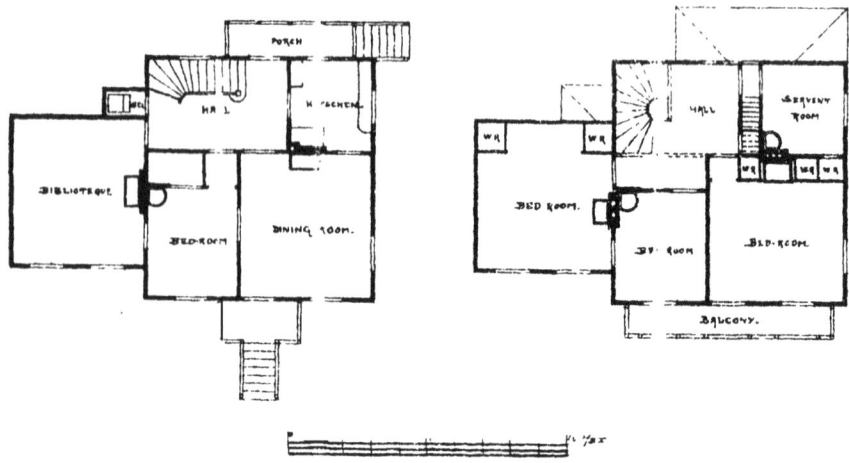

AKTIEBOLAGET
J.O. WENGSTRÖMS
MEK. SNICKERIFABRIK
STOCKHOLM.

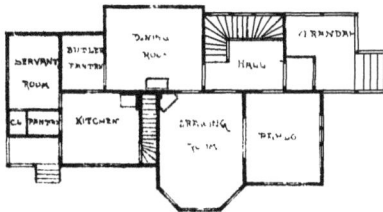

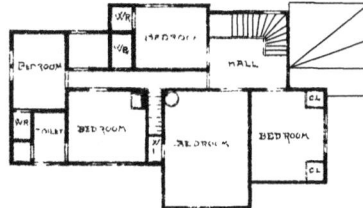

AKTIEBOLAGET
J. O. WENGSTRÖMS
MEK. SNICKERIFABRIK
STOCKHOLM.

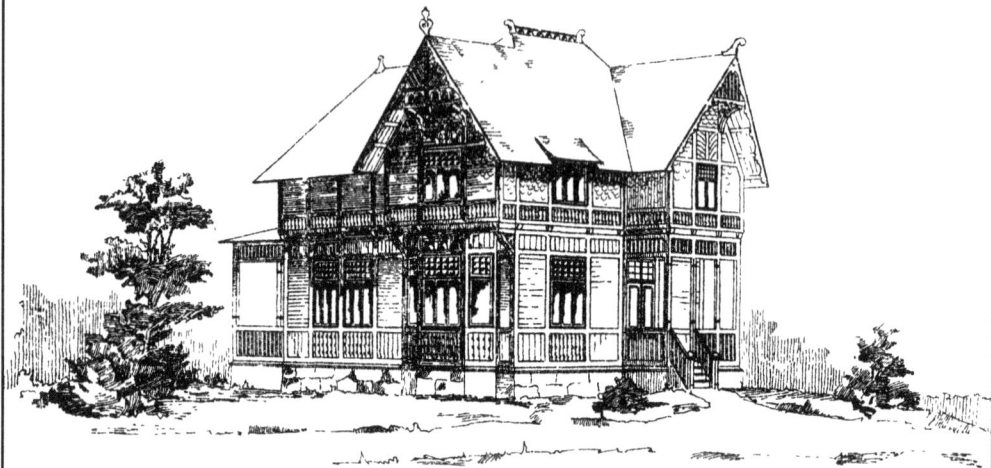

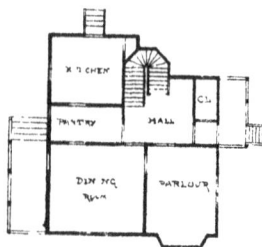

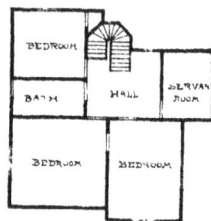

TRADE MARK

KITCHEN

C.L.

PANTRY   HALL

DINING   PARLOUR
ROOM

BEDROOM

BATH   HALL   SERVANT
ROOM

BEDROOM   BEDROOM

AKTIEBOLAGET
J.C. WENGSTRÖMS
MEK. SNICKERIFABRIK
STOCKHOLM.

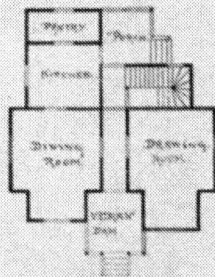

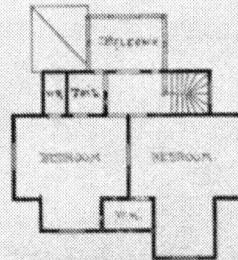

AKTIEBOLAGET
J.O.WENGSTRÖMS
MEK. SNICKERIFABRIK
,STOCKHOLM.

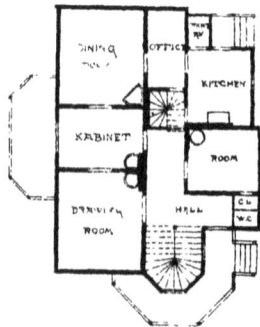

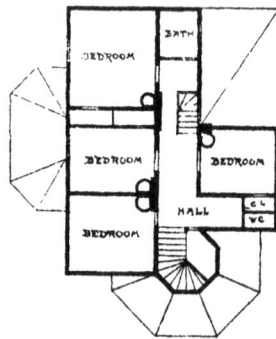

AKTIEBOLAGET
J.O.WENGSTRÖMS
MEK SNICKERIFABRIK
STOCKHOLM.

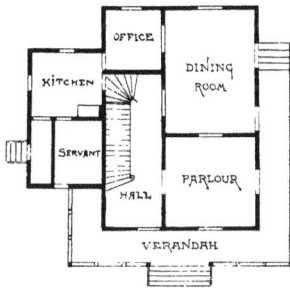

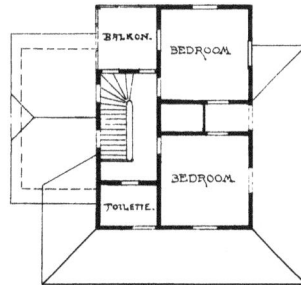

AKTIEBOLAGET
J.O.WENGSTRÖMS
MEK. SNICKERIFABRIK
STOCKHOLM.

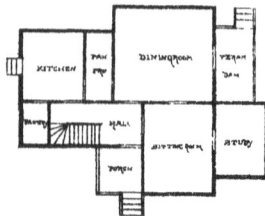

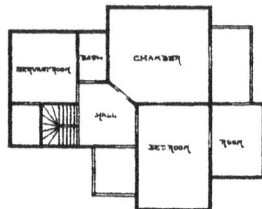

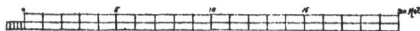

AKTIEBOLAGET
J.C.WENGSTROMS
MEK. SNICKERIFABRIK
STOCKHOLM.

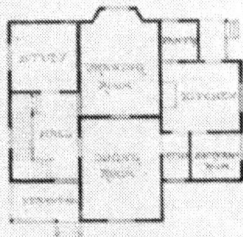

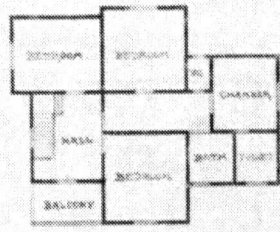

AKTIEBOLAGET
J.O.WENGSTRÖMS
MEK. SNICKERIFABRIK
STOCKHOLM.

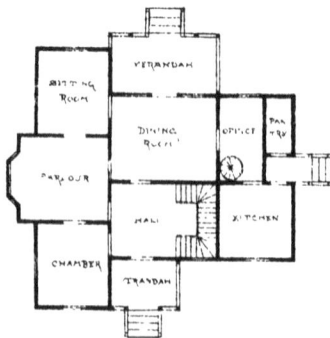

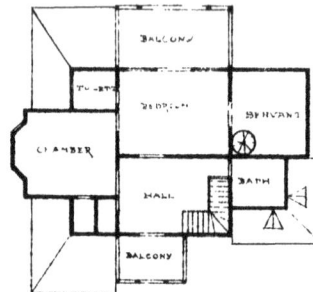

AKTIEBOLAGET
J.O.WENGSTRÖMS
MEK. SNICKERIFABRIK
STOCKHOLM.

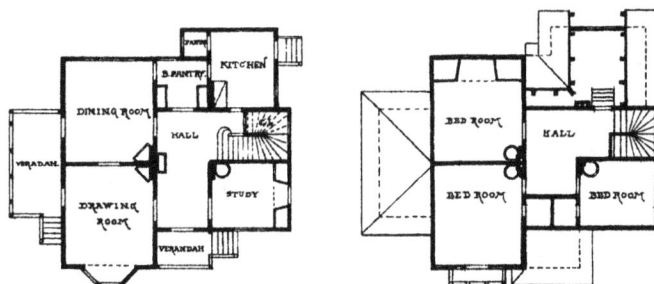

PANTRY

B.PANTRY   KITCHEN

DINING ROOM

HALL

VERANDAH

DRAWING ROOM

STUDY

VERANDAH

BED ROOM

HALL

BED ROOM

BED ROOM

0   5   10   15 Met

PL. 60.

AKTIEBOLAGET
J.O.WENGSTRÖMS
MEK. SNICKERIFABRIK
STOCKHOLM.

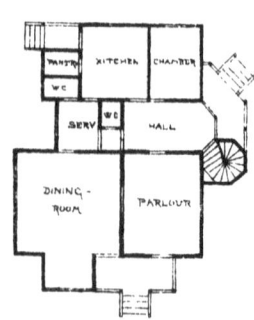

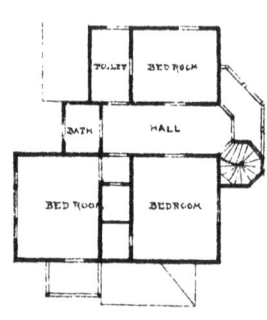

AKTIEBOLAGET
J.O.WENGSTRÖMS
MEK. SNICKERIFABRIK
STOCKHOLM.

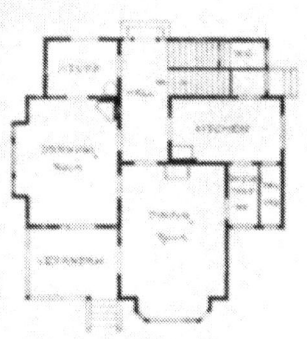

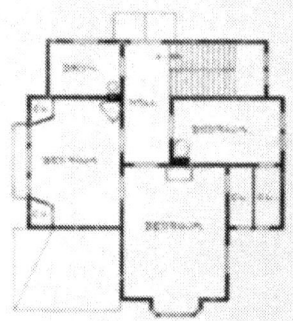

AKTIEBOLAGET
J.O.WENGSTRÖMS
MEK. SNICKERIFABRIK
STOCKHOLM.

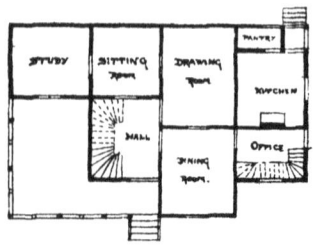

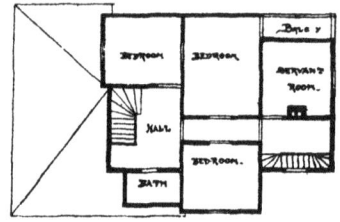

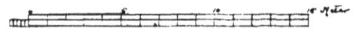

AKTIEBOLAGET
J.O.WENGSTRÖMS
MEK. SNICKERIFABRIK
STOCKHOLM.

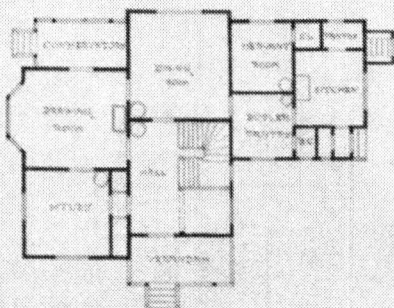

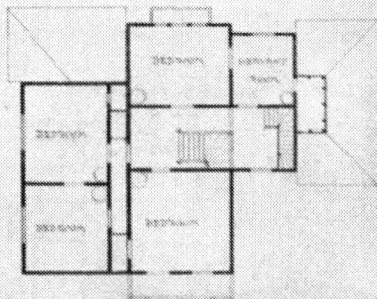

PL. 64.

AKTIEBOLAGET
J.O.WENGSTRÖMS
MEK. SNICKERIFABRIK
STOCKHOLM.

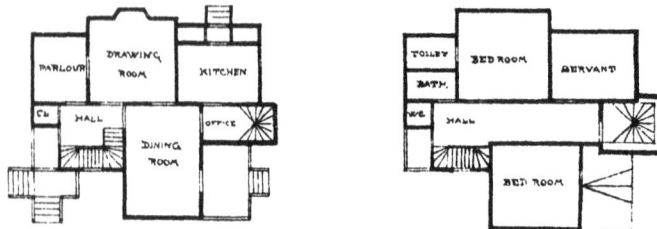

Ground floor plan:
PARLOUR · DRAWING ROOM · KITCHEN · CH · HALL · DINING ROOM · OFFICE

Upper floor plan:
TOILET · BED ROOM · SERVANT · BATH · WC · HALL · BED ROOM

AKTIEBOLAGET
J.O.WENGSTRÖMS
MEK. SNICKERIFABRIK
STOCKHOLM.

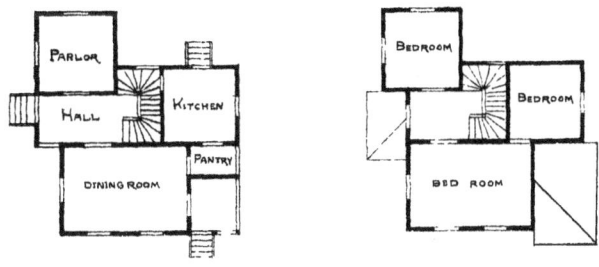

PARLOR

HALL   KITCHEN

PANTRY

DINING ROOM

BEDROOM

BEDROOM

BED ROOM

PL. 66.

AKTIEBOLAGET
J.O. WENGSTRÖMS
MEK. SNICKERIFABRIK
STOCKHOLM.

TRADE MARK

AKTIEBOLAGET
J.O. WENGSTRÖMS
MEK. SNICKERIFABRIK
STOCKHOLM.

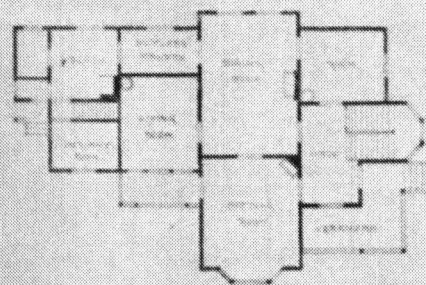

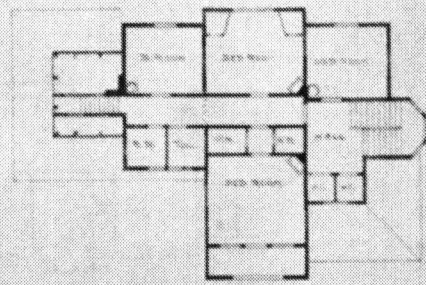

AKTIEBOLAGET
J.O.WENGSTRÖMS
MEK. SNICKERIFABRIK
STOCKHOLM.

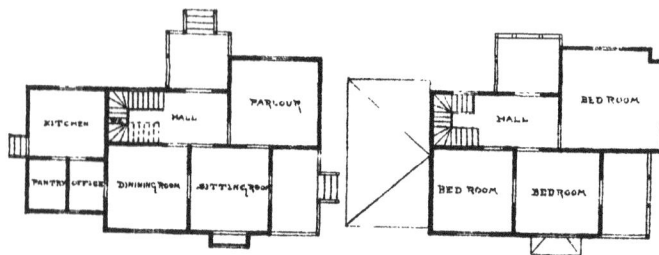

AKTIEBOLAGET
J.O.WENGSTRÖMS
MEK. SNICKERIFABRIK
STOCKHOLM.

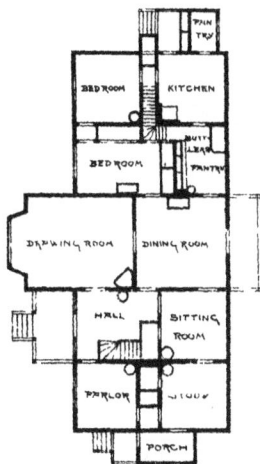

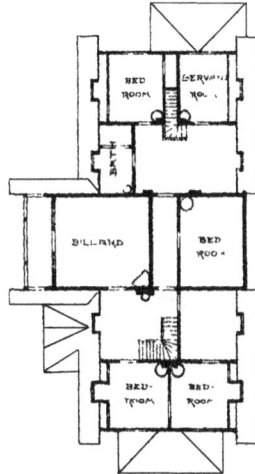

AKTIEBOLAGET
J.O.WENGSTRÖMS
MEK. SNICKERIFABRIK
STOCKHOLM.

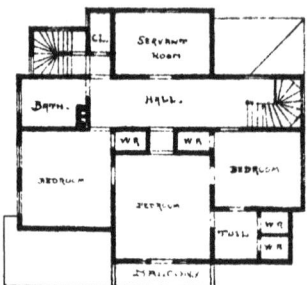

AKTIEBOLAGET
J.O.WENGSTRÖMS
MEK. SNICKERIFABRIK
STOCKHOLM.

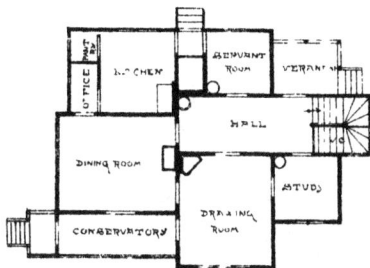

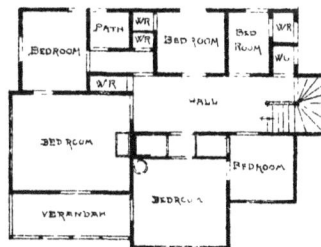

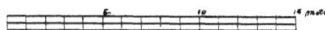

AKTIEBOLAGET
J.O.WENGSTRÖMS
MEK. SNICKERIFABRIK
STOCKHOLM.

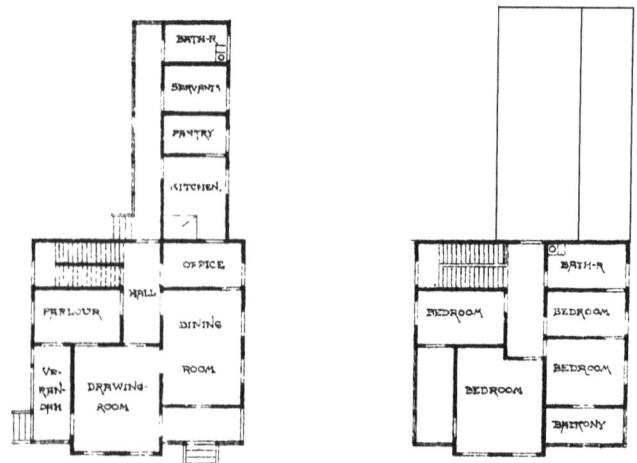

TRADE MARK

BATH-R
SERVANT
PANTRY
KITCHEN
OFFICE
PARLOUR
HALL
DINING
ROOM
VE-
RAN-
DAH
DRAWING-
ROOM

BATH-R
BEDROOM
BEDROOM
BEDROOM
BEDROOM
BALCONY

Pl. 73.

AKTIEBOLAGET
J. O. WENGSTRÖMS
MEK. SNICKERIFABRIK
STOCKHOLM.

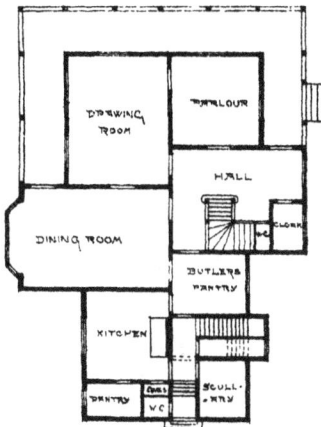

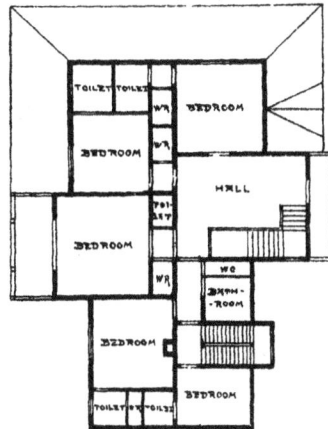

DRAWING ROOM

PARLOUR

HALL

DINING ROOM

CLOSET

BUTLERS PANTRY

KITCHEN

PANTRY COAL WC SCULL-ERY

TOILET TOILET WR BEDROOM

WR

BEDROOM

TOILET

HALL

BEDROOM

WR WC BATH-ROOM

BEDROOM

TOILET TOILET BEDROOM

5 MET

PL. 74.

AKTIEBOLAGET
J.O.WENGSTRÖMS
MEK.SNICKERIFABRIK
STOCKHOLM.

TRADE MARK

TRADE MARK

AKTIEBOLAGET
J.O.WENGSTRÖMS
MEK.SNICKERIFABRIK
STOCKHOLM.

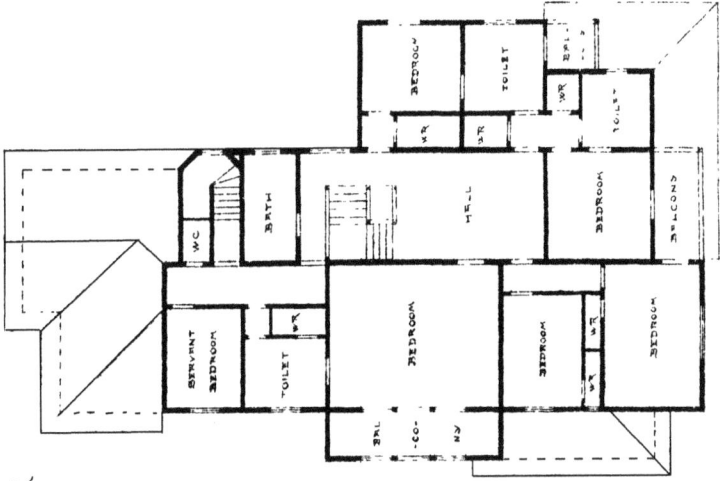

BEDROOM TOILET WR WR TOILET
WR R R BEDROOM VERANDA
WC HALL LIFT
SERVANT BEDROOM TOILET BEDROOM BEDROOM BEDROOM
BAL—CO—NY

BOUDOIR
CLOTH S CB
HALL VERANDAH
LIBRARY
DINING ROOM
DRAWING ROOM
CLO S
PANTRY
KITCHEN SERVANT

PL. 75.

TRADE MARK

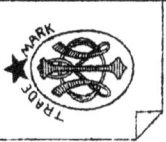

AKTIEBOLAGET
J.O.WENGSTRÖMS
MEK.SNICKERIFABRIK
STOCKHOLM.

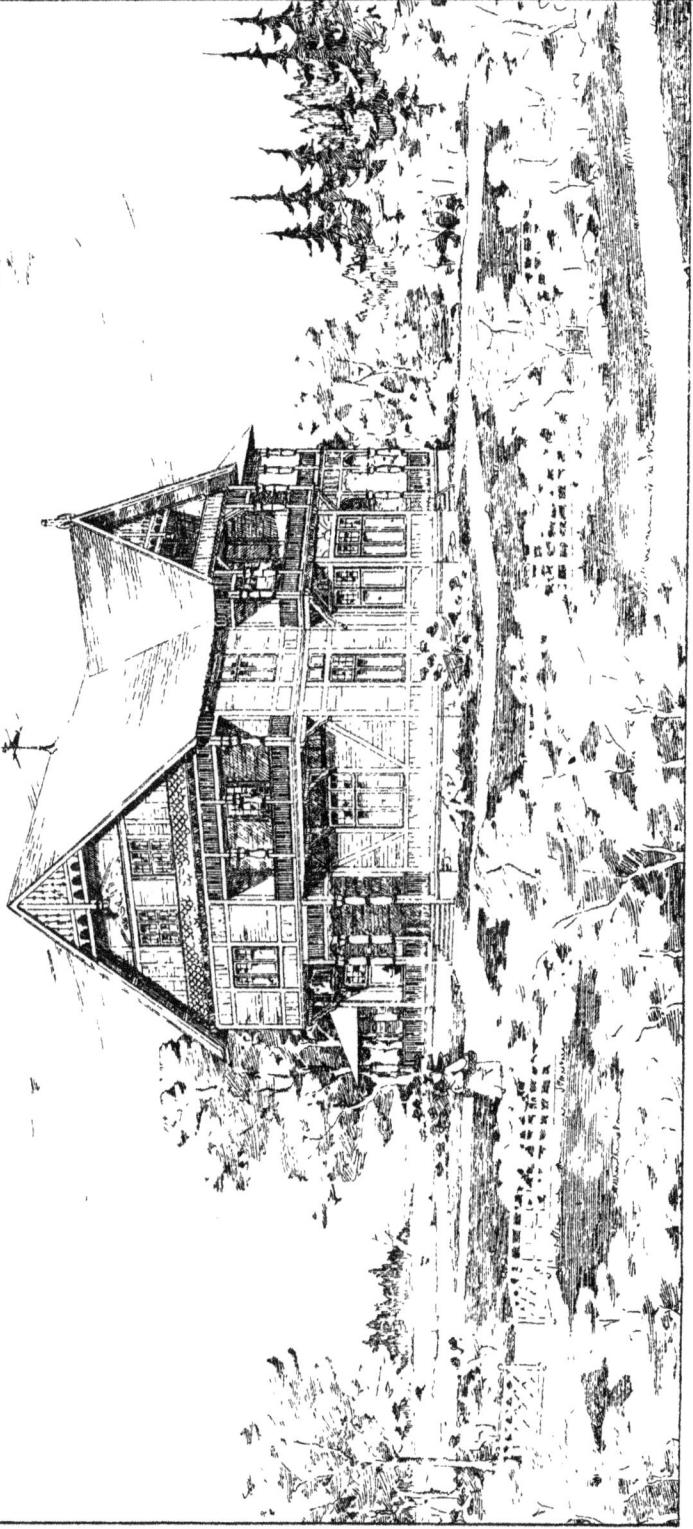

PL.75

TRADE MARK

AKTIEBOLAGET
J.O.WENGSTRÖMS
MEK.SNICKERIFABRIK
STOCKHOLM.

First floor plan:
BEDROOM
BATH
HALL
TOILET
WC
BEDROOM
BEDROOM
BALCONY
WR
WR
BEDROOM
BEDROOM
BALCONY
BALCONY

Ground floor plan:
BATH
SERVANT RM
PANTRY
KITCHEN
SERVICE ROOM
DINING ROOM
VERANDAH
HALL
DRAWING ROOM
VERAN DH
PARLOUR
CLOAKS

20 METR
10
5
0

AKTIEBOLAGET
J.O.WENGSTRÖMS
MEK. SNICKERIFABRIK
STOCKHOLM.

TRADE MARK

AKTIEBOLAGET
J.O.WENGSTRÖMS
MEK. SNICKERIFABRIK
STOCKHOLM.

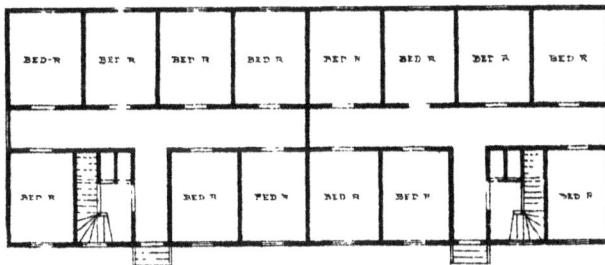

TRADE MARK

AKTIEBOLAGET
J.O. WENGSTRÖMS
MEK. SNICKERIFABRIK
STOCKHOLM.

AKTIEBOLAGET
J.O.WENGSTRÖMS
MEK. SNICKERIFABRIK
STOCKHOLM.

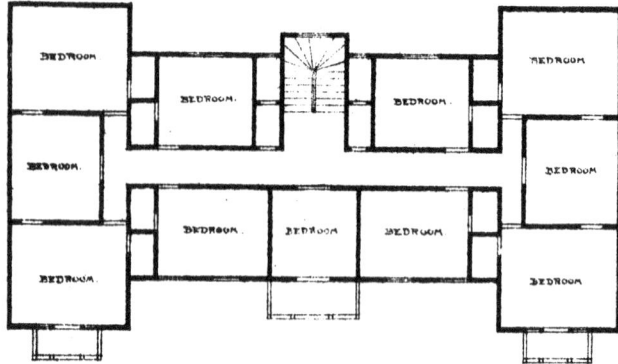

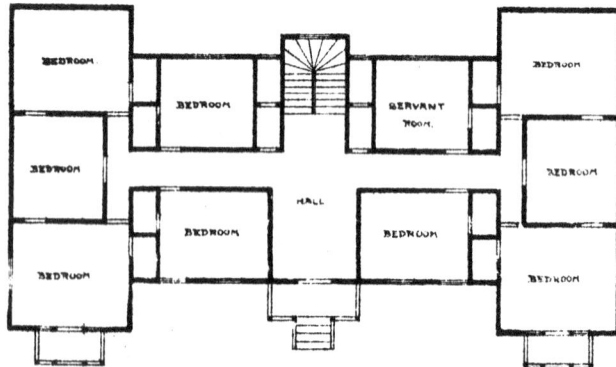

TRADE MARK

Upper floor plan:

BEDROOM | BEDROOM | BEDROOM | BEDROOM

BEDROOM | | | BEDROOM

BEDROOM | BEDROOM | BEDROOM | BEDROOM | BEDROOM

Lower floor plan:

BEDROOM | BEDROOM | SERVANT ROOM | BEDROOM

BEDROOM | | HALL | | BEDROOM

BEDROOM | BEDROOM | BEDROOM | BEDROOM

0   5   10   15   20 MET

PL. 78.

AKTIEBOLAGET
J.O.WENGSTRÖMS
MEK. SNICKERIFABRIK
STOCKHOLM.

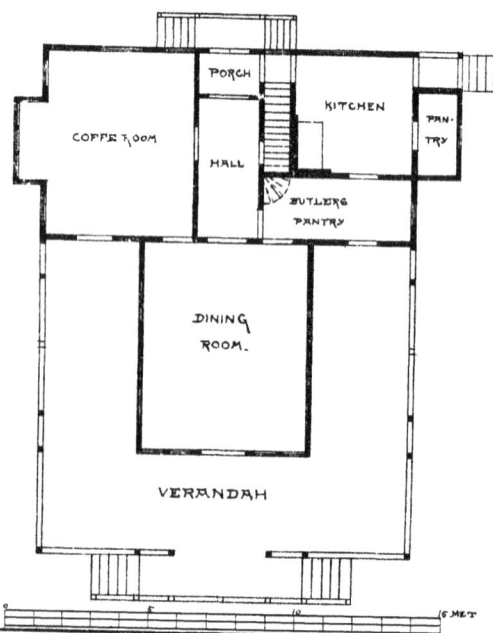

TRADE MARK

COFFE ROOM

PORCH

KITCHEN

PAN-
TRY

HALL

BUTLERS
PANTRY

DINING
ROOM.

VERANDAH

AKTIEBOLAGET
J.O. WENGSTRÖMS
MEK. SNICKERIFABRIK
STOCKHOLM.

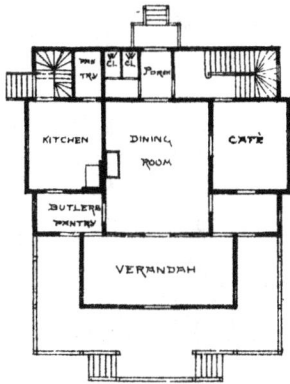

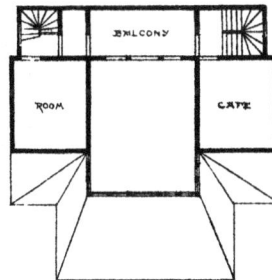

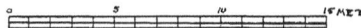

KITCHEN · DINING ROOM · CAFÉ · BUTLERS PANTRY · VERANDAH

ROOM · BALCONY · CAFÉ

0 · 5 · 10 · 15 MET

PL. 80.

TRADE MARK

AKTIEBOLAGET
J.O.WENGSTRÖMS
MEK.SNICKERIFABRIK
STOCKHOLM.

AKTIEBOLAGET
J.O.WENGSTRÖMS
MEK. SNICKERIFABRIK
STOCKHOLM.

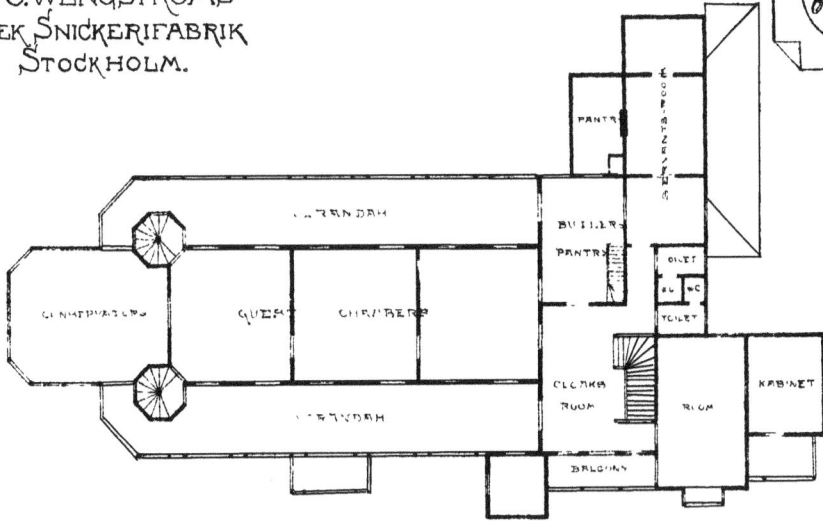

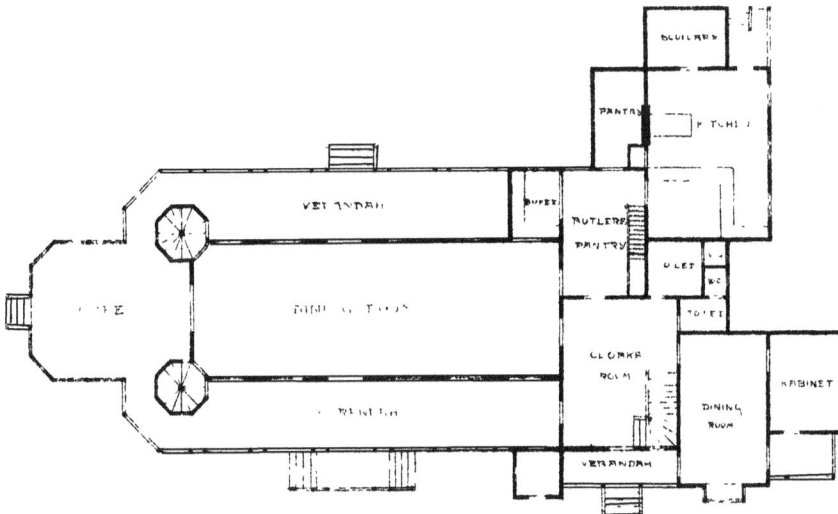

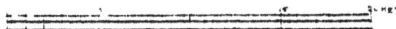

Pl. 81.

AKTIEBOLAGET
J.O.WÉNGSTRÖMS
MEK. SNICKERIFABRIK
STOCKHOLM.

TRADE MARK

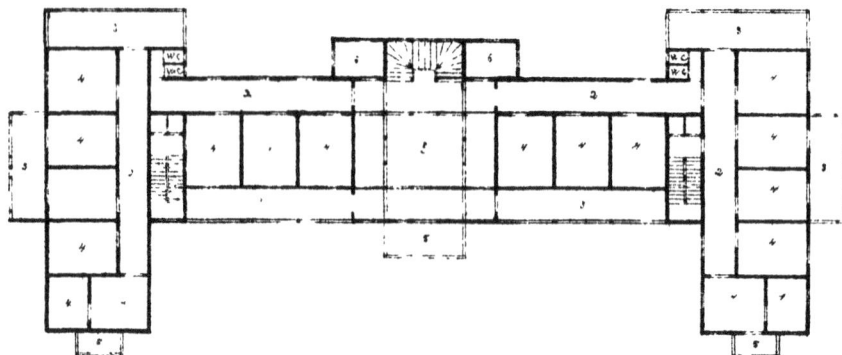

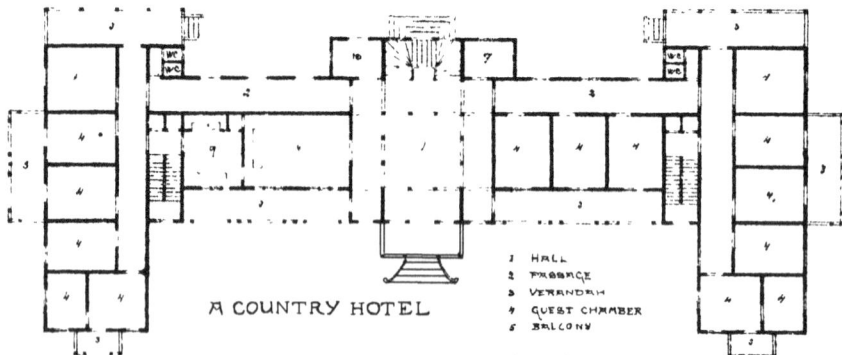

A COUNTRY HOTEL

1 HALL
2 PASSAGE
3 VERANDAH
4 GUEST CHAMBER
5 BALCONY

7 OFFICE
8 BREAK RETROOM
9 PANTRY
10 PORTIER

TRADE MARK

AKTIEBOLAGET
J.O. WENDSTRÖMS
MEK. SNICKERIFABRIK
STOCKHOLM.

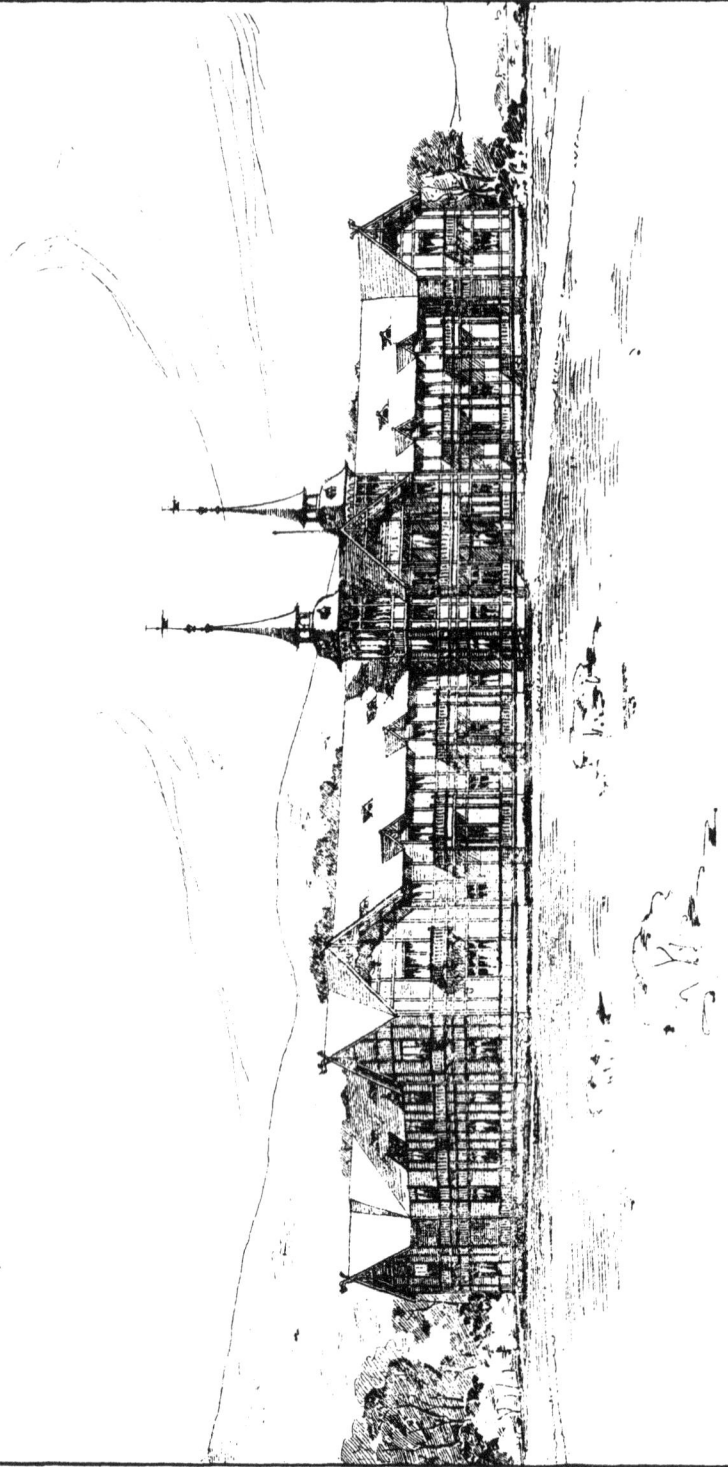

Pl. 82.

AKTIEBOLAGET
J.O.WENGSTRÖMS
MEK. SNICKERIFABRIK
STOCKHOLM.

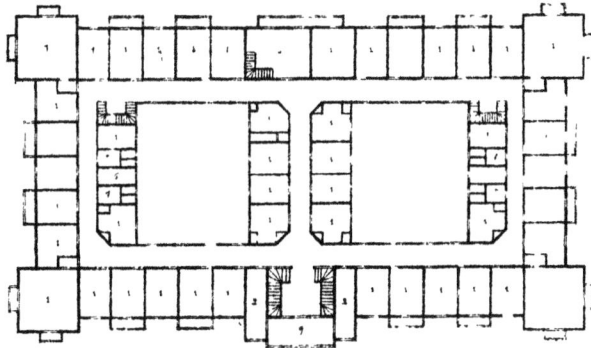

1 GUEST ROOM
2 SERVANT
3 PORTIER
4 OFFICE
5 KITCHEN
6 BATH ROOM
7 WATER CLOSET
8 CAFE
9 VERANDAH

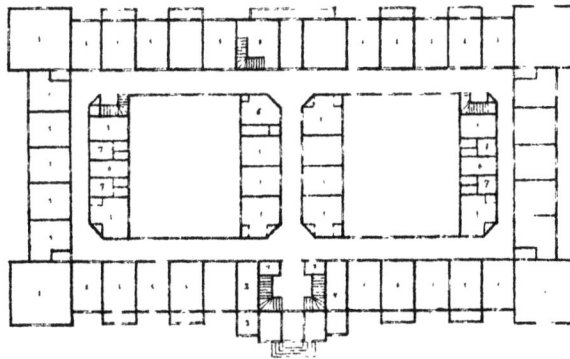

TRADE MARK

AKTIEBOLAGET
J.O. WENGSTRÖMS
MEK, SNICKERIFABRIK
STOCKHOLM.

AKTIEBOLAGET
J.Ö.WENGSTRÖMS
MEK.SNICKERIFABRIK
STOCKHOLM.

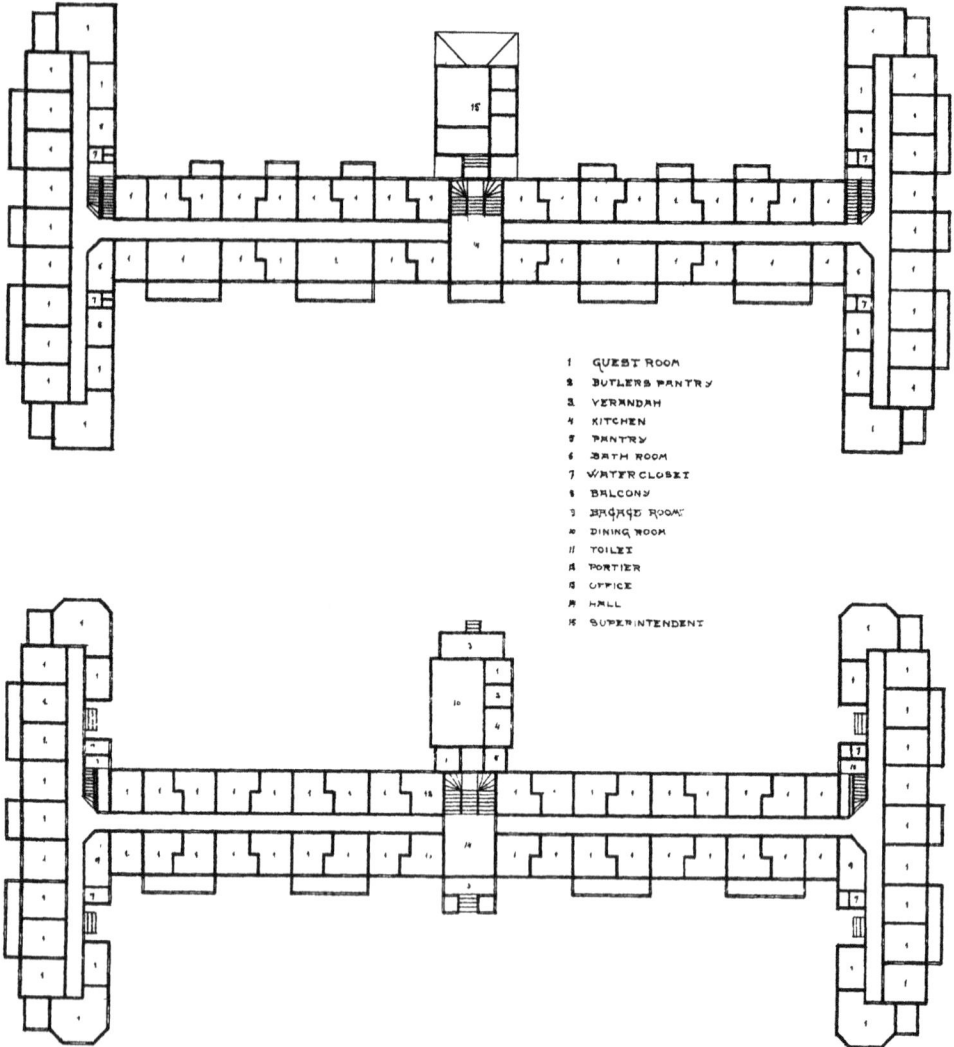

1   GUEST ROOM
2   BUTLERS PANTRY
3   VERANDAH
4   KITCHEN
5   PANTRY
6   BATH ROOM
7   WATER CLOSET
8   BALCONY
9   BAGAGE ROOM
10 DINING ROOM
11 TOILET
12 PORTIER
13 OFFICE
14 HALL
15 SUPERINTENDENT

AKTIEBOLAGET
J.O.WENGSTRÖMS
MEK.SNICKERIFABRIK
STOCKHOLM.

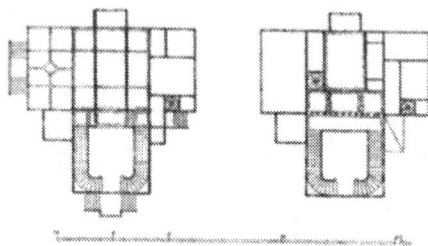

AKTIEBOLAGET
J.O. WENGSTRÖMS
MEK. SNICKERIFABRIK
STOCKHOLM.

www.ingramcontent.com/pod-product-compliance
Lightning Source LLC
Chambersburg PA
CBHW051225200326
41519CB00025B/7246